W9-ATY-038

Birthday & Relationship Digest
The Cards of Ilumination System

by Susan Hatahway and Debbie Crick

Copyright © 1998 in all countries of
the international copyright union.
All rights reserved, including the right to reproduce
this work in any form whatsoever.

Published by Illumination Enterprises.
For information write:
Cards of Illumination
P.O. Box 770, Sedona, AZ 86339
FAX (520) 204-1544

ISBN 0-9655631-5-4

Rachlin Publishing Group
215 West 90th St.
Suite 2c NYC 10024

Illustration: Pam Fullerton Miller
Design and Typography: Gopa Design

This book is also available in a deluxe
hardbound edition for $24. Contact your local bookstore

We would like to acknowledge
our teachers for their intense love
and study of the Card System:

TABLE OF CONTENTS

DIAMONDS

SPADES

THE JOKER

RELATIONSHIPS

ILLUMINATION
THROUGH THE CARDS

laying cards are one of the most globally recognized symbols in existence. Virtually every
home has a deck. In medieval times, when
paper was widely used for the first time, the original playing cards were developed as a way of safeguarding an even
more ancient system. This system dated back to ancient
Egypt and the Far East, but was in danger of being destroy-
ed. Therefore the masters at the time decided to "hide" the
information in a form that could be given out to many,
hence the deck of cards. Little has changed over the years
in a simple deck of playing cards, and fortunately the information contained remained unchanged and preserved to
be made available today.

The Cards of Illumination system is based on Olney H.
Richmond's Mystic Test Book, originally published in
1893, and others. The elegance of its mathematical preci-
sion is evident in the fact that the data is contained in 52
cards; which corresponds to the number of weeks in a year;
12 royal cards, the number of months in a year; and the 4
suits, the number of seasons, the four astrological elements
(fire, earth, air and water) as well as the weeks in a month.

Everyone in the world is represented by one of the
cards in a deck. The birth card for each birthday can be

found on the Birth Chart at the beginning of the book.

The Birth Card, which is similar to the zodiac sign, is the most important symbols of who we are and represents our individualism and significance. Through our Birth Card we can discover many aspects of our personality, as well as trials and limitations, our gifts and opportunities, professional tendencies, hidden strengths and much more. All cards have both challenges and blessings in any given lifetime and no one card is superior to any other.

Understanding our relationships, whether romantic or professional is greatly enhanced by using this system. We can see what type of partner we might be attracted to, and how we may relate to specific connections. Using the composite of two Birth Cards (by adding two Solar Values together), we can gain insight on different aspects of any relationship.

ABOUT THE AUTHORS

Susan Hathaway and Debbie Crick are students and teachers of the card system and co-founders of Cards of Illumination located in Sedona, AZ. Their intention is for this instrument to be made available to anyone who has the desire to learn. They offer seminars, workshops and products to assist those who are interested in the study of this ancient system.

Card Calendar
The Cards of Illumination System

Find Your Birth Card
The Cards of Illumination System

DAY	JAN	FEB	MAR	APR	MAY	JUN	JUL	AUG	SEP	OCT	NOV	DEC
1	K♠	J♠	9♠	7♠	5♠	3♠	A♠	Q♦	10♦	8♦	6♦	4♦
2	Q♠	10♠	8♠	6♠	4♠	2♠	K♦	J♦	9♦	7♦	5♦	3♦
3	J♠	9♠	7♠	5♠	3♠	A♠	Q♦	10♦	8♦	6♦	4♦	2♦
4	10♠	8♠	6♠	4♠	2♠	K♦	J♦	9♦	7♦	5♦	3♦	A♦
5	9♠	7♠	5♠	3♠	A♠	Q♦	10♦	8♦	6♦	4♦	2♦	K♣
6	8♠	6♠	4♠	2♠	K♦	J♦	9♦	7♦	5♦	3♦	A♦	Q♣
7	7♠	5♠	3♠	A♠	Q♦	10♦	8♦	6♦	4♦	2♦	K♣	J♣
8	6♠	4♠	2♠	K♦	J♦	9♦	7♦	5♦	3♦	A♦	Q♣	10♣
9	5♠	3♠	A♠	Q♦	10♦	8♦	6♦	4♦	2♦	K♣	J♣	9♣
10	4♠	2♠	K♦	J♦	9♦	7♦	5♦	3♦	A♦	Q♣	10♣	8♣
11	3♠	A♠	Q♦	10♦	8♦	6♦	4♦	2♦	K♣	J♣	9♣	7♣
12	2♠	K♦	J♦	9♦	7♦	5♦	3♦	A♦	Q♣	10♣	8♣	6♣
13	A♠	Q♦	10♦	8♦	6♦	4♦	2♦	K♣	J♣	9♣	7♣	5♣
14	K♦	J♦	9♦	7♦	5♦	3♦	A♦	Q♣	10♣	8♣	6♣	4♣
15	Q♦	10♦	8♦	6♦	4♦	2♦	K♣	J♣	9♣	7♣	5♣	3♣
16	J♦	9♦	7♦	5♦	3♦	A♦	Q♣	10♣	8♣	6♣	4♣	2♣
17	10♦	8♦	6♦	4♦	2♦	K♣	J♣	9♣	7♣	5♣	3♣	A♣
18	9♦	7♦	5♦	3♦	A♦	Q♣	10♣	8♣	6♣	4♣	2♣	K♥
19	8♦	6♦	4♦	2♦	K♣	J♣	9♣	7♣	5♣	3♣	A♣	Q♥
20	7♦	5♦	3♦	A♦	Q♣	10♣	8♣	6♣	4♣	2♣	K♥	J♥
21	6♦	4♦	2♦	K♣	J♣	9♣	7♣	5♣	3♣	A♣	Q♥	10♥
22	5♦	3♦	A♦	Q♣	10♣	8♣	6♣	4♣	2♣	K♥	J♥	9♥
23	4♦	2♦	K♣	J♣	9♣	7♣	5♣	3♣	A♣	Q♥	10♥	8♥
24	3♦	A♦	Q♣	10♣	8♣	6♣	4♣	2♣	K♥	J♥	9♥	7♥
25	2♦	K♣	J♣	9♣	7♣	5♣	3♣	A♣	Q♥	10♥	8♥	6♥
26	A♦	Q♣	10♣	8♣	6♣	4♣	2♣	K♥	J♥	9♥	7♥	5♥
27	K♣	J♣	9♣	7♣	5♣	3♣	A♣	Q♥	10♥	8♥	6♥	4♥
28	Q♣	10♣	8♣	6♣	4♣	2♣	K♥	J♥	9♥	7♥	5♥	3♥
29	J♣		7♣	5♣	3♣	A♣	Q♥	10♥	8♥	6♥	4♥	2♥
30	10♣		6♣	4♣	2♣	K♥	J♥	9♥	7♥	5♥	3♥	A♥
31	9♣		5♣		A♣		10♥	8♥		4♥		JOK

HEARTS

This suit is primarily concerned
with understanding life through relationships.
People are most important in their life.
Love, family, creativity, emotion
and youth are key heart words.

HEARTS

NEW LOVE CARD

You desire new love, new beginnings and are creative. Self-worth, passion and expression are important to you. You had a strong maternal influence for ill or for good. You have a keen mind for new financial endeavors. Your challenge is selfishness or jealousy. You can be a loner or could see yourself as "number one". You have a pioneering heart, are ambitious and could be creative when applying financial schemes. Your networking ability in the community is strong and you could make a large contribution to public causes. Your restless heart could lead to much emotional change. Many career opportunities are open to you by expressing your creative mental talents, such as writing. Illness may occur when inner stress leads to anger or financial worries. Often there are disappointments in personal relationships. To release any skeptical beliefs around ideologies, and have mastery over self, a change in values must be accepted.

A ♥
BIRTHDAY

12/30

LOVE & COOPERATION

You desire love, cooperation and harmony in relationships. You are curious, enjoy learning and are a seeker of knowledge. You want ease and comfort. You are kind, devoted, soft and have tendencies toward self-indulgence. You may struggle with the idea of being independent and the desire of union in a relationship. You gravitate to a strong mate and have a keen mind. You have had a strong parental influence. You were born with a knack for writing and communicating. Romance is a big part of you and often many compromises are made in relationships. Earth-related occupations could prove to be beneficial throughout your life. Caution is advised when dealing with financial partnerships. You have high ideals of love and marriage, and are sometimes unrealistic. Inspiration may be tapped through the theater and music. Your challenges around finances must be carefully handled so as not to affect your well-being.

2 ♥
BIRTHDAYS
12/29

LOVE CHOICE

*Y*ou love the stage and performing, and will most likely incorporate music into your life's work. You have the need to satisfy yourself and may use your varied experiences to determine your boundaries. You have a curiosity to satisfy, and constantly hunger for new knowledge. Nurturing others through service and communication is important to you. Your intuition can be of utmost value to yourself and others throughout your life. Hard work often meets with recognition and success. You have strength available to overcome any obstacle. Use your restlessness for the benefits of your varied interests and career opportunities. You must be very responsible in paying all debts, or indecision regarding your values will affect your bank account and your health. Through many changes and closures in your lifetime, you have the opportunity to master yourself.

3 ♥
BIRTHDAYS
11/30, 12/28

SECURITY & PROTECTION IN LOVE

You desire emotional security and often create a strong heart connection with family and friends. You love your home, your family and your country. You are lucky with money, cooperate well with others and do well in groups. You have a strong sense of justice, tolerance and understanding. You have a tendency to be controlling and set in your ways. Your loving and intensely sensitive ways often attract others for their own healing. Be cautious when establishing your protection that you do not isolate yourself. With so much emotional charm and charisma, you are at your best when involved in group related activities. You can have a 'stick-to-it' attitude that can prove to be very productive, especially in your middle years of life. Once you determine your life's mission, many may benefit from your ways. Through using your intuition and serving others, much richness, both spiritual and material, will be yours.

4 ♥
B I R T H D A Y S
10/31, 11/29, 12/27

13

EMOTIONAL CHANGES

You love new, unusual people, places and things. You require a variety of interests, are changeable and want to experience many of life's offerings. You are often athletic, as you love sports. Often you travel and move away from where you grew up. You can be lucky with money and always have enough to take care of your needs. Traveling for business may bring financial security. Watch the tendency to make speculative investments, as you like to take risks. Making up your mind is not an easy task, especially concerning your love nature. You are attracted to intelligent, creative and spontaneous mates. Often there are disappointments with males in your life. By letting go of negative beliefs, you are able to create and benefit financially. By releasing and transforming issues around anger, you are able to create balance in your material and spiritual life.

5 ♥
B I R T H D A Y S
10/30, 11/28, 12/26

MISSION OF LOVE

You desire a stable heart. A priority in your life is maintaining peace in all your personal relationships. Giving to others is your mission, and you tend to make compromises in relationships for the sake of harmony and balance. With your stable, constructive mind, counseling comes naturally. You are good with numbers and computers. You are witty and have a delightful sense of humor. It is no wonder that your charm appeals to many. You benefit greatly from fields pertaining to communication and metaphysical studies. The ability to learn anything is yours if you avoid static conditions which you may have created in your life. Often you have tests around time and money. Avoid being lazy, as you reap what you sow. This is the Christmas Day card and your life is intended to be full of giving and receiving the gifts of love.

6 ♥
BIRTHDAYS
10/29, 11/27, 12/25

UNCONDITIONAL LOVE CARD

You need to learn to release and let go of all expectations in your relationships. You are interested in things of the past and of a precious nature. You are refined, reserved and sensitive. You have much love to give to the world. Many counselors and teachers are this card, as there is the ability to emotionally heal others. Letting go of any heart-related fears will bring victory to your spirit. Your charm and charisma create much power socially and with groups, especially for promoting. Often you need to let go of fears around money and material security. You may find traveling and changes in your lifestyle rewarding, as they may satisfy your restlessness. Frequently there are many completions and closures in your life. Because of your sensitivity, you must be careful in health related matters. Through releasing negative mental patterns, you are initiated into a new level of awareness.

7 ♥

BIRTHDAYS:

9/30, 10/28, 11/26, 12/24

16

LOVE HEALER

You are socially charming, love groups, are popular and generous. You express much power through emotional persuasion, if you tap into your inherent wisdom. You have power to overcome all obstacles. Your strong emotions must be used for the benefit of humanity and not used selfishly. There is much vitality and aggression in pursuit of romance. Blessings and opportunities come to you through successfully developing your mental capacities. You are challenged to be responsible in work and health. You could be attracted to teaching or healing professions and be successful financially. You have tremendous leadership qualities, but your authority could be overbearing. Be careful not to bully. Use care with decisions regarding your heart, as they may lead to disillusion in romance.

8 ♥
BIRTHDAYS
8/31, 9/29, 10/27, 11/25, 12/23

UNIVERSAL GIVING

Throughout your life you have many emotional fulfillments and many closures. You are compassionate, have a good memory, and often have a good sense of humor. You receive many gifts through inspired thoughts and revolutionary thinking. A career in communication, education, publishing or writing may prove to be lucrative for you. Anything of a speculative nature, such as gambling, may prove to be detrimental to your well-being. You may have many completions regarding matters of the heart. You enjoy travel. Since relationships may cause financial burdens, take heed that your restless emotional nature does not become a financial burden to you. You enter this life with many things and people you need to let go of. Much strength is yours to endure emotional giving. You want personal love, but you belong to the universe.

9 ♥

BIRTHDAYS:

8/30, 9/28, 10/26, 11/24, 12/22

PROMOTERS CARD

❧

*Y*ou are social, independent and charming. As a Heart, you work well with the public and groups. Often you receive recognition for your efforts. You can work well with children as they enjoy you. You are not afraid of hard work. You do well in positions of authority and can be assertive. Your drive for material success is strong, although your spending is too. Your basic health pattern is generally good. You often mask your sensitivity with a confident facade. Your ambitious drive must be followed with patience and discipline. You may need change, variety and travel to satisfy your restless emotional nature. Expression of your mental creativity is important throughout your life. Getting in touch with your anger and releasing negative thought patterns could change your values. Success comes through awareness of your inner self, hard work, and organizational abilities.

10 ♥
BIRTHDAYS

7/31, 8/29, 9/27, 10/25, 11/23, 12/21

Universal Love Card

You are self-sacrificing and a powerful spiritual influence. You are stubborn. You can be teacher or messenger for the masses. This card is the symbol of the Christ principal. You often sacrifice much in your life for higher beliefs. You suffer if you do not give. You are an initiator for a higher heart. You can be successful in a position of authority and often are attracted to humanitarian pursuits. Many blessings are yours through mastering your emotions. You need to be aware of codependency. Keeping a clear mind and not letting your strong emotional nature interfere is important for you. Your great mental awareness increases on your spiritual path through the years. You love children and they love you. Your challenge in life is learning to cooperate in all dealings, especially for financial benefit. Be mature and responsible.

J♥

BIRTHDAYS

7/30, 8/28, 9/26, 10/24, 11/22, 12/20

QUEEN OF LOVE

This is one of the marriage cards. It represents romance. You wear the crown for being loving, nurturing and romantic. You love luxury. You can be creative, very ambitious and have a good mind for financial success. You experience life though your heart and emotions. You enjoy traveling. It is important for you to realize that self indulgence, laziness and control could be your downfall. Often your relationships can be bumpy. You have a keen mind for educational pursuits and others would benefit through this knowledge. You have the ability to overcome any diversities life offers. Your blessings have to do with the variety of people you meet. It is important for you to create solid boundaries. Using your intuition for humanitarian pursuits serves you and others well. Your challenge is being able to change your philosophies and ideas. Be versatile and giving.

Q ♥
BIRTHDAYS
7/29, 8/27, 9/25, 10/23, 11/21, 12/19

MASTER OF THE HEART

You have strong emotion and romantic power. You are ruled by love. You are here to master your emotions through relationships. You had a strong father influence for ill or for good. You can be an ideal parent and romantic partner. You have a tendency to intellectualize your feelings. It is often necessary for you to make compromises and adjustments for the sake of harmony in your relationships. You have a good mind for business and can wear the crown of authority when it comes to management or self-employment. You have a tendency to be practical and thorough in business. Through joining forces in financial partnership you receive many business opportunities. Through the test of discipline and awareness you can have direct experience into the mystery of life. It is important for you to remember that loving yourself is the most precious gift of all.

K ♥
B I R T H D A Y S

6/30, 7/28, 8/26, 9/24, 10/22, 11/20, 12/18

CLUBS

*This suit is primarily concerned
with understanding life through communication.
Seeking information through mental
processes is their quest.
Knowledge, logic, mental intuition
and education are key club words.*

CLUBS

New Knowledge

❦

You are curious about life and desire information. It is important for you to share this knowledge with others. You are a pioneer, creative, freedom loving, independent, and love ideas and communication. At a very early age you started accumulating information of all forms. You have a receptive mind and enjoy working hard and usually receive recognition for it. You had a strong maternal influence for ill or for good. You are challenged to release any fears and expectations regarding romantic relationships. Your charisma serves you well in public life. Personally it is often a challenge. Emotional completions and closures play an important role in your life. Transformation occurs for you through travel, and many changes regarding your lifestyle. Caution not to be so self involved that you miss the boat.

A ♣
BIRTHDAYS
5/31, 6/29, 7/27, 8/25,
9/23, 10/21, 11/19, 12/17

THE COMMUNICATOR

You enjoy great conversation and sharing ideas. Cooperation in communication is what you strive for. You are detail-oriented, changeable, diplomatic and have a fear of being alone. Your early years were strongly influenced by your father. You have an intuitive mind and a great ability to master much knowledge. You like to have fun, be creative and could be prone to a sensitive stomach. A great deal of your vitality comes from security in love and marriage. Luck runs high for you financially as you are, most likely, protected. Often there are challenges with your health. When accessing your powerful emotions, you have great success in charming the public. You have a strong intuition. Sharing your ideas, by teaching others, helps to expel many of your fears. By integrating your tremendous wisdom and power you have the ability to see the truth.

2♣
BIRTHDAYS
5/30, 6/28, 7/26, 8/24,
9/22, 10/20, 11/18, 12/16

MENTAL CREATIVITY

❧

You can best express your gift of mental creativity through writing. Financial opportunities are many. You have a variety of careers to choose from in your lifetime. Management or owning your own business is common. Travel for financial gain often satisfies your restless spirit. To experience your love fulfillment you need to decide what you want in relationships. Try not to compromise. Discipline your mind for a positive attitude. By releasing and letting go of negative mental patterns you can draw material success to yourself. There are opportunities for business ventures through travel. Fluctuating finances are no stranger to you. A woman in your life may be the cause of some financial burden. You can be fun-loving and like to be mentally stimulating. Through family, friendship and loving support, you are able to experience emotional security.

3 ♣
BIRTHDAYS
5/29, 6/27, 7/25, 8/23,
9/21, 10/19, 11/17, 12/15

MENTALLY STRONG

You have a practical mind and are a builder of ideas. You can be stubborn and will go to great lengths to create stability. You are down-to earth, diplomatic, practical and have a wealth of knowledge. You have a heightened sense about people. You have a keen mind for sales, financial deals, and dealings with the community. Early in life your mother played a dominant role. Education is important in order to harness your great intellectual potential. Your financial blessings and opportunities come from consistent and basic values. Usually you have much protection around your health. By being out in public and working with organizations and groups of people, you experience success. Your later years are often filled with financial blessings. Recognition and success come from your ability to work hard.

4 ♣
BIRTHDAYS
4/30, 5/28, 6/26, 7/24,
8/22, 9/20, 10/18, 11/16, 12/14

VERSATILE MIND

❧

*Y*ou are spontaneous, love freedom and welcome change. You are progressive, intellectual, versatile and often skeptical. You must express yourself. You have a mind for creativity with finances. While you may appear open and communicative, you are emotionally secretive in regard to your personal life. Often you are a digger for the truth. Traveling temporarily satisfies your restlessness. Your blessings and opportunities occur when you release fears involving relationships and material abundance. Avoiding commitment is common. You often make sacrifices for humanitarian pursuits. By overcoming the many closures, fulfillments and endings in your life, you are able to be open to having close intimate relationships. By having mastery of your emotional nature you are able to experience peace and harmony in love.

5 ♣
BIRTHDAYS

3/31, 4/29, 5/27, 6/25, 7/23,
8/21, 9/19, 10/17, 11/15, 12/13

THE MESSENGER

Y ou have deep knowing of and a responsibility to truth. You can bring knowledge and light to others once you determine what your message is. You have a desire for information, are creative, love ease, comfort, music and harmony. You are here to learn that whatever you give, you will get back. You can be lazy and irresponsible. Your home and your family are important to you. You have the power to overcome all health obstacles in a natural way, and usually have robust vitality. You can be a networker in the community. You have a strong desire for teaching, learning, the stage, sciences and spiritual pursuits. Your challenge is to trust and rely on your inner guidance. Much wisdom is available you; use it to enlighten your fellow man and to pave the way for others.

6 ♣
BIRTHDAYS

3/30, 4/28, 5/26, 6/24, 7/22,
8/20, 9/18, 10/16, 11/14, 12/12

INTUITIONAL POWER

❧

You have the gift of gab and love conversation. You generally have a good sense of humor and a quick mind. You can be both mentally inspired and inspiring. You have good money potential and a strong spending urge. Releasing negative thoughts and ideas is no stranger to you. Listening to your inner voice creates faith, hope and trust. You often have a cherub face and can light up the room with your presence. You have strong organizational skills which you probably learned from your influential mother. Your blessings and opportunities often come from investments, especially from real estate. Through positive thinking, your health will benefit. When working with the public or groups, your emotional power can heal many. By recognizing your great inner knowledge and mastering your mental potential, you can communicate enlightenment to many others.

7♣
BIRTHDAYS
3/29, 4/27, 5/25, 6/23, 7/21,
8/19, 9/17, 10/15, 11/13, 12/11

MENTAL STRENGTH

You have mental power to accomplish anything. You are stubborn and set in your ways. Once you have made up your mind you are rarely influenced by others. You like to work and build foundations. You are great with children because you can be very nurturing. Balance in all areas of your life is essential. You have much vitality to access the public and people-related endeavors. Much financial success occurs when service to others is emphasized. Because of your powerful mental strength, be careful not to bully others. You have great intuitive gifts available to heal yourself and others. Often you have an attraction for unusual partners in love and friendships. Patience and flexibility are qualities that need to be developed in order to sustain healthy relationships. Your later years may include travel, adventure, and writing.

8 ♣
BIRTHDAYS

3/28, 4/26, 5/24, 6/22, 7/20,
8/18, 9/16, 10/14, 11/12, 12/10

Universal Thinker

❧

*Y*ou enjoy offering ideas that appeal on a universal level. You are curious, intelligent and love adventure. Service related fields are what you are suited for best. Romance is often foremost on your mind. You enjoy an intelligent conversation. Watch for codependency in your relationships. Be willing to take chances and keep your mind clear. Your greatest challenges may be around letting go of ideas and beliefs that no longer serve you. Be careful that your strong, sensual, emotional nature does not take precedence in your life. Your blessings and opportunities come from assuming positions of authority and activities related to public service. By accessing your gifts with the public, a great deal of healing, recognition and success are possible. Take care to be responsible in all areas of your life, for what you sow, you shall surely reap.

9 ♣
BIRTHDAYS

1/31, 2/29, 3/27, 4/25, 5/23,
6/21, 7/19, 8/17, 9/15, 10/13, 11/11, 12/9

KNOWLEDGE CARD

❧

You love to receive and share knowledge. This is the teacher's card. You have a great mind for finances and detail. You may be attracted to healing professions. You probably had a very strong mother influence. A strong life partner would be most suited to you. You do well in the limelight and often receive success and recognition for your hard work. You sometimes have so much on your mind, you may have difficulty sleeping. You can be creative and attracted to drama or music. Emotional indecisiveness may make it difficult to make a commitment. You have much intuition, but often do not accept or recognize this gift. Service can be the most rewarding of all your experiences. Because of your strong intellectual nature, your emotional nature is often neglected – Get in touch.

10♣
BIRTHDAYS

1/30, 2/28, 3/26, 4/24, 5/22, 6/20,
7/18, 8/16, 9/14, 10/12, 11/10, 12/8

MENTALLY INSPIRED

✦

*Y*ou have many successful ideas through revelations. You are stubborn, independent, creative and spontaneous. You are well-suited for being out in the public. One of your talents is being creative around financial resourcefulness. You love a good conversation. It is very important that your mate is intelligent and also enjoys communication. One of your strongest gifts is your intuition, which serves you well in business, sales and other opportunities. Many benefits come through humanitarian pursuits. You love to have fun. Through work and self discipline, your financial efforts are rewarded. Your blessings and opportunities are many if you accept the responsibility of authority. Be careful not to be too critical of yourself and others. Throughout your life you attract unusual people and circumstances. Through service, inspiration and ideals, you wear the crown of love.

J ♣
BIRTHDAYS

1/29, 2/27, 3/25, 4/23, 5/21,
6/19, 7/17, 8/15, 9/13, 10/11, 11/9, 12/7

Intuitive Knowledge

❧

You know from the Source, so always listen to your inner voice and be receptive to higher knowledge. Your intuition is one of the strongest of all the cards. You have a strong mind for hard work and can receive recognition for it. You can be high-strung, creative and reactive. You can be quite clever regarding finances and do well when you are the boss, or in a management position. You are freedom-loving, and can be drawn to spiritual studies. You enjoy variety and have an unsatisfied quest for knowledge. You could be successful at writing, publishing and service related careers. One of your tests in life may have to do with understanding unconditional love in relationships. Inheritance is probable at some time in your life. Promotion, travel, and change of lifestyle are familiar to you. Your challenge is to get in touch with your emotions.

Q♣
BIRTHDAYS
1/28, 2/26, 3/24, 4/22, 5/20,
6/18, 7/16, 8/14, 9/12, 10/10, 11/08, 12/06

MASTER OF THE MIND

You are the master communicator and successful in all mental areas. You live by your intuition, are creative and have powerful emotions. You are good at all forms of communicating, including publishing, writing, sales and education. You can wear the crown when it comes to leadership. You have a keen mind and are often a futuristic thinker. You have a very romantic heart. Family is the utmost of your priorities, yet often your greatest challenge. Partnership and cooperation provide great opportunity and blessings for you along your life path. You are psychically brilliant, curious and always learning and teaching others. You are a Knower and Seeker of the truth. It is important for you to establish solid boundaries in all relationships. By honoring and loving yourself you are able to express from your heart. 'Freedom' is your battle cry.

K♣
BIRTHDAYS

1/27, 2/25, 3/23, 4/21, 5/19,
6/17, 7/15, 8/13, 9/11, 10/9, 11/7, 12/5

DIAMONDS

This suit is primarily concerned
with understanding life through values.
Acquiring worth, both material
and immaterial are essential.
Systems, evaluation, financial matters
and business are key diamonds words.

DIAMONDS

New Financial Idea

*Y*ou are curious, independent and outgoing. Your big question is: love or money? You had a strong, dominating female early in life. You have a keen mind for beginning new financial endeavors. Material gain is a powerful influence, yet yearning for love is just as strong. Your love nature leans toward emotional restlessness or, perhaps, movement that leads to travel and change. You can be idealistic. You have many thoughts that could involve mental indecision, worry or confusion. Use this mental influence for creative endeavors like writing, publishing, theatrical pursuits and other forms of communication. Your blessings occur through expressing your artistic talents. Relationship disappointments and completions are your tests. You have a big heart when it comes to giving. During your lifetime many changes occur regarding your value system.

A ◆
BIRTHDAYS

1/26, 2/24, 3/22, 4/20, 5/18,
6/16, 7/14, 8/12, 9/10, 10/8, 11/6, 12/4

FINANCIAL DEAL

Y ou are good at solving problems. You can be original with ideas for new financial endeavors. In the community, you are instrumental in being the link and have much power with people. You are attracted to a mate of intelligence. Often you are in relationships for financial security. You are an independent thinker and have innate intuition when it comes to people and situations. Often you are fearful of being ripped off. You are a natural with the computer. It is important for you to set definite goals. You have strong endurance. You do well in groups, are comfortable in the limelight, and enjoy traveling. Your sense of humor makes you quite charming. Fear of change often keeps you in a situation longer than need be. It is important for you to be in touch with your emotions. Your blessings come through solid work and practical application.

2◆
BIRTHDAYS
1/25, 2/23, 3/21, 4/19, 5/17,
6/15, 7/13, 8/11, 9/9, 10/7, 11/5, 12/3

CREATIVE FINANCE

Yu have more experiences on your life path that teach you about values, than others. You can make money from a variety of sources. Spending may be an issue with you. You are very bright and can be very indecisive at times. Often you are involved in relationships of a fated nature that involve many adjustments and compromises. Much growth happens for you through travel, career and people-related activities. Your challenge is the need to develop independence. Sacrifice through service assists you in lightening your load. A positive attitude will go a long way in aiding you through disappointments. Most of your challenges occur around romantic relationships. Your lesson in life is to have mastery of your financial affairs. Creativity or indecision? The choice is up to you.

3 ◆
BIRTHDAYS

1/24, 2/22, 3/20, 4/18, 5/16,
6/14, 7/12, 8/10, 9/8, 10/6, 11/4, 12/2

PROTECTED FINANCE CARD

All your life you are financially protected as long as you apply yourself through hard work. An inner restlessness often causes you impatience. You are an independent thinker and can cooperate with many types of people. Your charm and charisma are one of your greatest attributes. You are very sweet, with much intuition and sensitivity. Blessings and opportunities come to you through your ability to persevere in any situation. Females, children and marriage may prove to be your tests, therefore your greatest rewards. Your great understanding of higher truth is initiated when demonstrating leadership abilities. Through self mastery and awareness, material success is promised to you. Your challenge in life is to integrate and realize your tremendous power and wisdom.

4 ◆
BIRTHDAYS

1/23, 2/21, 3/19, 4/17, 5/15,
6/13, 7/11, 8/9, 9/7, 10/5, 11/3, 12/1

FLUCTUATION IN VALUES

You are spontaneous, energetic, friendly, charitable and creative. A career involving sales could prove beneficial. Your independent nature is freedom-loving. You are intuitive. Change of lifestyle is common. You must learn to let go of fear, worry and uncertainty in your life. You seldom live near your place of birth. You are comfortable working with groups. Your mother has been very influential in your life. Often you are athletic. You crave change, variety and new opportunities. You are attracted to mates who are strong, creative and mentally inspirational. Caution regarding speculative ventures, such as gambling, even though you are lucky. Learning to communicate and be cooperative is your test as well as your reward. Learn to trust your strong intuitive instinct.

5 ◆
BIRTHDAYS

1/22, 2/20, 3/18, 4/16, 5/14,
6/12, 7/10, 8/8, 9/6, 10/4, 11/2

FINANCIAL PAY BACK

❧

*M*uch of your life is about settlement of your debts, financial and value related. You can overcome most obstacles associated with your early childhood. You attract many unusual, interesting people into your life. Often you choose to create space for yourself. You have the talent, energy and ability to create much material success in your life. Your blessings and opportunities come through your ability to heal others by your presence and your power with groups of people. Often you have anger that you need to deal with. Your tests in life come through your great desire for love, affection and self-fulfillment. Your natural inclination toward religion and philosophy supports incredible intuitional abilities. On an emotional level, you have many completions. By letting go of negative ideas, you create success inwardly and outwardly: As above so below.

6 ◆
BIRTHDAYS
1/21, 2/19, 3/17, 4/15, 5/13,
6/11, 7/9, 8/7, 9/5, 10/3, 11/1

VICTORY THROUGH FAITH

※

his card has been called the millionaire's card. When you learn to let go of your fears around money and adopt an 'attitude of gratitude' material abundance is yours. It is important for you to develop balance in your material and spiritual life. Early on in life, curiosity and travel tickle your fancy. It is common occurrence that you are likely to inherit money, although it often comes with losses around a female family member or mate. You sacrifice much for your family. You aggressively pursue romance. Closures, endings and completions in your life are often opportunities in disguise. Your strong personal desire for that ideal romance often tests you to your limit. This test and challenge may spur you on to a greater love for humanity. By developing your incredible mental powers and learning to focus, you can manifest and create anything you set your mind to.

7 ◆
BIRTHDAYS
1/20, 2/18, 3/16, 4/14,
5/12, 6/10, 7/8, 8/6, 9/4, 10/2

FINANCIAL REWARD

*Y*ou like to shine and be the center of attention. This is the card of making and spending money. Being organized is a high priority. You have a very powerful mind and a good memory. Your father, in early years, was a powerful influence. Indecision and variety often create havoc in your love life. You are aggressive in pursing new information as it helps satisfy your tremendous curiosity about life. Your blessings and opportunities come through using your intuition, being a good communicator, and any field to do with publishing. Through hard work and responsibility you receive success and recognition in your chosen field. Often you change your mind, and "freedom" is your battle cry. Many challenges in your life have to do with changes in your lifestyle. You can be skeptical at times, so pick up the load and lighten up!

8 ♦
BIRTHDAYS
1/19, 2/17, 3/15, 4/13,
5/11, 6/9, 7/7, 8/5, 9/3, 10/1

THE GIVER

⁂

You have a passion to begin new projects. Throughout your life there will be many. You have a very broad and humanitarian vision of life. You can be extravagant in your tastes and you like to spend. Managing your money is not an easy task for you. You are good at sales and have a great mind for putting deals together. You are attracted to intelligent people and like to have a partner to share and communicate with. Emotionally, you are family oriented. You have positive dealings with most men in your life and legal affairs are usually beneficial for you. Many creative ideas around finances occur for you and some time in your life you are likely to have quite a bundle. Real estate and land ventures are profitable. Using your charisma and tremendous emotional power helps you achieve your mission. Teaching and sharing your universal knowledge has a transforming effect on your life.

9 ◆
BIRTHDAYS
1/18, 2/16, 3/14,
4/12, 5/10, 6/8, 7/6, 8/4, 9/2

MONEY CARD

*Y*ou are financially protected as long as you recognize service. You do well in life dealing with large-scale business and handling large sums of money, yours or others. Many of you are stockbrokers, bankers or enjoy management. Your high value system can affect many if you choose a service oriented career such as teaching, counseling, children, etc. Your materialism may be undermined by your strong desire for love and affection. Your vitality often is fed by creative ways of making money. Your blessings and opportunities come through mastering your finances and your values. Beware of your often extravagant taste, since you do like to spend. A strong female often proves beneficial at some point in your life. Many of your challenges involve emotional restlessness, uncertainty and change. By giving of yourself to humanity, you achieve the peace and satisfaction you so desire.

10♦
BIRTHDAYS
1/17, 2/15, 3/13, 4/11, 5/9, 6/7, 7/5, 8/3, 9/1

INSPIRATIONAL IDEA

*Y*ou are creative, idealistic, original and great in sales. You want money and always know how to get it. You have an electrical mind and are capable of coming up with great money-making ideas. You are a combination of highly material and highly spiritual. Your integrity may be challenged, so beware of dishonesty. You are truly fun-loving, youthful and love to shop. Even though you are freedom-loving, you do better in partnership. Partnership provides stimulus for you to be more creative and productive. Using your wit and charm, you can be very effective in any profession that deals with healing. You are sensitive and intuitive. Your challenge is not to get so caught up with everyday occurrences that you ignore your inherent spiritual gifts. Avoid being lazy. You are likely to have many positive personal experiences while traveling. Your challenge is balancing spirituality and materialism.

J ◆
BIRTHDAYS

1/16, 2/14, 3/12, 4/10, 5/8, 6/6, 7/4, 8/2

48

RECEPTIVE TO HIGHER VALUES

You have a good business sense and love to spend money. You are called upon to develop a high value system through many of life's tests. Learning to depend upon yourself is one of life's greatest lessons for you. The more you give universally, the more you are able to receive personally. Your restless heart keeps you forever on the go and you love to travel afar. Leadership is your strong suit. It is generally recognized by many at a very early age that you can wear the crown. Use your mental creativity positively so it does not turn into indecision and worry. In your later years, travel and foreign interests may satisfy a need for your freedom-loving nature. You experience many tests through relationships. By releasing negative mental patterns that fetter your mind, you are able to tap into and master your knowledge and intuition.

Q ◆
BIRTHDAYS
1/15, 2/13, 3/11, 4/9, 5/7, 6/5, 7/3, 8/1

AUTHORITY IN VALUES

ecause you wear the crown, you need to own your business or be in a management position. You have a keen business sense, are creative when it comes to writing and can be extremely stubborn. You are the only 'one-eyed king' and often see things only one way, your way. You have a strong desire for mental pursuits, writing and communication. Curious in love, you seek partners of intelligence. You can be aggressive in financial pursuits, especially with men. Your blessings and opportunities come through inspiration and revelation. Your challenge in life is to focus and discipline your mind in order to achieve success. Promotion of self is not your strongest suit. Financial advancement occurs when public relations are pursued. Your strong, independent ways often interfere with cooperation in partnership for financial gain. Humanitarian service brings great spiritual and material rewards.

K ♦
BIRTHDAYS

1/14, 2/12, 3/10, 4/8, 5/6, 6/4, 7/2

SPADES

*This suit is primarily concerned
with understanding life through work.
Transformation occurs when there
is a balance with career and spirituality.
Labor, health, wisdom and intuition
are key spades words.*

SPADES

TRANSFORMATION

You are creative and at your best when focused on work. On some levels you can be a loner and very private. You are ambitious, secretive, driven and mystical. Your powerful card has been chosen to represent this card system because it symbolizes the mystery of life. It has also been chosen by playing card companies all over the world as their trademark as it is a very powerful symbol. Due to your charismatic nature you attract a variety of interesting people to yourself. Often there are fears regarding relationships. You are attracted to people of financial worth and have, yourself, a strong desire for the finer things of life. Much travel and movement are stimulating for you. Despite difficulties, when you focus on humanitarian pursuits, peace and satisfaction are yours to experience. When in deep water, become a diver.

A ♠
BIRTHDAYS
1/13, 2/11, 3/9, 4/7, 5/5, 6/3, 7/1

PARTNERSHIP IN WORK

You can influence the public and you are often found influencing them at large. Balance occurs best when you listen and are open to the sounds around you. Cooperation in work is your forte. "Freedom" is your battle cry. You are charismatic and have tremendous power with groups. You have a keen mind for business and finance. Career choices are often unusual, but can bring financial success when working with the public. Communication is essential in all your relationships. Your beliefs are stronger than your feelings. Romance is often fated. Indecision in love and romance is challenging for you. Emotionally you may find satisfaction and recognition in your work. Traveling, versatility and changes of lifestyle bring you mental satisfaction. Expression is important, as it makes your life lighter.

2 ♠
BIRTHDAYS
1/12, 2/10, 3/08, 4/06, 5/04, 6/02

INTERNAL ENERGY

You are super-creative and abundance comes when you are ready to work. If you do the work, you get the rewards. You should let go of negative ideas and mental patterns that keep your mind cluttered, because you must have mental freedom. You are restless and have a lot of energy. Caution is advised not to spread yourself too thin regarding work or health, as this can lead to worry and stress. Athletics come naturally to you. Adhere to the law when it comes to your values and all financial dealings. You have many blessings that come through women. When it comes to your career, concentrate on your organizational skills. Success in business occurs when your creativity is in line with your ideals. You are emotionally protected and feel secure with a loving family. You have a tendency to be critical of yourself. Lighten up!

3♠
BIRTHDAYS
1/11, 2/09, 3/07, 4/05, 5/03, 6/01

GOOD SUPPLY OF WORK

You are a hard worker. A solid sense of family and relationship is important to your well-being. You have a powerful, healing and calming effect on others. You receive your greatest satisfaction in work and health. Healing professions are most successful, either natural or conventional. You work well in group situations. You are successful when industrious. You may be attracted to influential females that could bring monetary success. You must develop a higher sense of values and realize that your consistency and discipline will be rewarded. You have a strong desire for money and can be very charitable. Success comes from benefiting others. Originality for invention is strong. Your universal lesson is in giving to humanity. You must learn to release any negative ideas or belief patterns connected to your emotions. By doing that you will have a total change of values.

4 ♠

BIRTHDAYS

1/10, 2/8, 3/6, 4/4, 5/2

CHANGE IN LIFESTYLE

Y ou are restless, artistic and work best in groups. You enjoy being on the go! Travel, sales and promoting are often key factors in your life. Often in early years, sacrifice related to a male relative was experienced. Work related to humanity comes natural to you. Business partnerships are beneficial, yet cooperation must be achieved at all costs. Heart-related lessons may come often and emotional mastery will greatly improve your well-being. You may have successful dealings with real estate. You have charm that appeals to the public and it will be vital in assisting people in lifestyle changes. You are very intuitive and love peace and harmony. Mental stability is a challenge for you. Many lessons deal with honesty and spirituality. The ultimate outcome of your individual life plan has to do with a mission of enlightening yourself and others through higher knowledge.

5 ♠
BIRTHDAYS
1/9, 2/7, 3/5, 4/3, 5/1

RESPONSIBILITY IN WORK

This is a very strong card. You have the ability to overcome all obstacles in your path. You can be a great universal giver and a humanitarian. You have a mission to lead others to their true lifestyle. Romance can sometimes cause disillusion and indecision. Your mate must be educated. In business, great opportunity and power is available, but often in your emotional life there is much indecision. You have a lot of energy to manifest large sums of money. Futuristic and unusual ideas are often at your disposal. Your intuition is strong if you heed it. Your challenge is balancing your involvement in work and success, with your strong desire for love and emotional support. By letting go of emotional expectations and fears around relationships, you experience victory.

6 ♠
BIRTHDAYS
1/8, 2/6, 3/4, 4/2

57

SPIRITUAL LIFESTYLE

Y̶ou have a good mind for conversation and are curious in seeking the mysteries of life. You are popular with the public, charming and sociable. You do your best work in partnership for the benefit of mankind. You can handle large sums of money and are at your best when self-employed. You are attracted to unusual, intelligent, strong mates. You have much energy to put into financial creativity and sales. Blessings and opportunities come to you through your marriage and hard work. You have many tests around believing that you are financially protected. You are very charitable and have a desire for higher knowledge. Use your charisma to your own benefit when dealing with large groups of people. Your challenge is balancing your inner and outer worlds, staying on the path and recognizing your mission in life. Your transformation will occur through service to others.

7 ♠
BIRTHDAYS
1/7, 2/5, 3/3, 4/1

THE HEALER

You have much power available to you through the healing professions. You attain many blessings through hard work, discipline, responsibility and working with large groups of people. You have the inner strength to overcome the many obstacles that life offers you. By using caution you may avoid a tendency to be excessively concerned with yourself and your desires. You may satisfy your restless heart by traveling or change of residence. Your lessons include keeping focused to tap into your tremendous creativity. By giving on a universal level, your monetary affairs will benefit. Self-mastery and service are your lessons. Release negative mental patterns that fetter your mind. Through right thinking you will draw material abundance to yourself. Your transformation comes by being receptive to higher universal values.

8 ♠
BIRTHDAYS
1/6, 2/4, 3/2

COMPLETION IN LIFESTYLE

You are the strongest of all the nines. In your life you have many endings, lifestyle transitions and completions. Your focus needs to be universal. You have a mind for knowledge and new information. You are curious and can be skeptical. Regardless of your gender, a wise man has assisted you in some way. You have the desire to handle large amounts of money and be self-employed or in a management position. Blessings and opportunities are yours by being emotionally stable and staying on course. You have much creative, artistic and acting ability that can be used in teaching others about their spirituality. You are very original, unconventional, like to work and can be idealistic. It is important for you to realize that all debts be recognized and cleared before spiritual progress can be achieved. You have a powerful, sensitive emotional nature. Learn to use this as a vehicle to higher truth.

9♠
BIRTHDAYS
1/5, 2/3, 3/1

PROSPERITY THROUGH LABOR

ou enjoy hard work and usually receive recognition for it. Your drive for work and success can interfere with your relationships and home life. You appear to be independent, but are not happy alone. You are mentally alert and it is often difficult for you to focus your restless mind. Often in your love nature, your insecurity creates disharmony because of your emphasis on material values. You are curious and often seek to know the answers to life on a very deep level. Your life is most rewarding when you get in touch with your strong emotional nature. You are advised to use caution in regard to any secret dealings. Your opportunities come from letting go of expectations or fears of abandonment in relationships. You have a powerful charismatic nature. Use it wisely. Higher awareness comes through closures, fulfillments and service.

10♠
BIRTHDAYS

1/4, 2/2

REVELATION THROUGH LABOR

*S*aint or devil, the choice is yours. Throughout your life, many lessons will present themselves to you to exercise your discernment and honesty. You have an incredible mind, and your ability for mental focus is exceptionally strong. It is important for you to be realistic and responsible concerning your values. You reap what you sow. Your vitality and productivity are often protected. People contacts bring you much success, both socially and professionally. Tests come to you through responsibility and hard work. Medicine, acting, science, farming, music and mysticism are some of the careers that can stimulate your creativity and bring you monetary rewards. You have the power to overcome most difficulties, especially with your health. It is important for you to release deep seated anger and replace it with your tremendous creativity.

J♠
BIRTHDAYS

1/3, 2/1

MASTERY OF SELF

You are the card of self mastery. Your organizational skills accompany you to wear your crown in authoritative positions. You are a hard worker and are often self-employed. You have a strong, quick, aggressive mind. You appreciate quality and often do not consider the price. Through service to others you can succeed in both the spiritual and mundane worlds. You have strong intuitional powers. Knowledge and communication may be your biggest blessings in helping to release your fears. You have a creative mind for many careers that could lead to singing, acting, sales and, perhaps, writing. Building a solid sense of values may personally challenge you at different times in your life. Learning balance and cooperation in all relationships, both personal and working, is extremely important on your life path.

Q♠

BIRTHDAY

1 / 2

THE MASTER

You are the master. You are wise, powerful and can wear the crown of authority better than anyone else in the deck. If you use your stubbornness to your advantage, you can be quite forceful in realizing your tremendous potential. Dealing with change is often difficult for you to accept. You are creative and impatient and often have a strong mental focus. Emotionally, you are often indecisive and uncertain in your relationships. You are attracted to a partner that is a good communicator. Your intuition can be one of your greatest allies. By applying yourself through your unique talents and capabilities, recognition is guaranteed. Your restless mental nature may prove to be a major challenge for you. Through releasing emotional and financial fears, you can achieve mastery in all aspects of your life.

K♠
BIRTHDAY

1 / 1

JOKER

Mathematically, this jovial, legendary figure

does not have an assignment in this system.

He makes his own rules and mirrors others.

Strength, practicality, wisdom and

mystery are joker key words.

JOKER

THE JOKER

Being the only non-traditional card of the deck, you make your own rules. Your keen wit aids in the many choices in your life path, as there are many. You are youthful, independent, personable, productive, and have a good mind for business. You often are seeking that special romantic partner that you like to have fun with. You have many trials and choices around love matters. You can master much and often do best in a management, or in a self-employed position. You relate to the outdoors and often feel grounded making your profession doing earth related work. Expressing yourself creatively is important to you. In relationships it is essential that your partner is sincere. Practicality, endurance and stability are strong influences for you. You can be the irresponsible fool, or the deeply spiritual initiate. The choice is yours.

JOKER
BIRTHDAY

12/31

RELATIONSHIPS

 here are many variables that contribute to the success of a relationship. However, the cards never take away our individual choices. Free will is always a factor. By discovering more about our relationships, we are able to better understand them. A relationship can be most successful if both partners want it and are willing to work toward mutual priorities and goals.

FINDING THE SOLAR VALUE OF A RELATIONSHIP:

There are different values assigned to each of the cards. To find the value of a relationship, using the Solar Value Chart, simply add the two different card values together to create a composite or relationship card.

EXAMPLES:

April 28 = 6♣ = Solar Value 19
May 17 = 2♦ = Solar Value 28
19 + 28 = 47 is the 8♠

When the total is larger than 52,
you must then subtract the total from 52.

July 3 = Q♦ = Solar Value 38
Aug 13 = K♣ = Solar Value 26
38 + 26 = 64   64-52 = 12, the Q♥

This allows us to see at a glance what the relationship is about. The following descriptions will give a summary of the essence of the relationship and the challenges and blessings that might occur.

NOTE: Anytime we have a relationship with someone born December 31 (the Joker, with a solar value of 0), when we add our solar value to it, the relationship always turns out to be our own card. This relationship is a reflection of ourselves. Whatever we like or dislike about ourselves is mirrored back to us. This also occurs with a K♠, which has a Solar Value of 52.

OUR RELATED CARDS

The essence of our characteristics can be found in our Birth Cards. However, we all have either one or two other cards we are related to. These related cards are another facet of ourselves and our personalities. You can learn more about yourself when you examine these other Related Birth Cards. If you have friends, family or lovers that your card is related to, you will find that there is a very strong bond between you.

OUR RELATED CARDS
(see explanation at left)

A ♥ = A ♦, 3 ♥   A ♦ = 2 ♦, A ♥
2 ♥ = A ♣   2 ♦ = 6 ♣, A ♦
3 ♥ = A ♥, Q ♣   3 ♦ = 6 ♥, Q ♦
4 ♥ = 4 ♠, 10 ♠   4 ♦ = 5 ♠, 5 ♥
5 ♥ = 4 ♦, 5 ♣   5 ♦ = 9 ♦, 3 ♣
6 ♥ = 4 ♣, 3 ♦   6 ♦ = 9 ♣, 3 ♠
7 ♥ = 8 ♥, A ♠   7 ♦ = 9 ♥
8 ♥ = 7 ♥, 7 ♠   8 ♦ = Q ♠, 7 ♣
9 ♥ = 7 ♦   9 ♦ = Q ♦, 5 ♦
10 ♥ = J ♣, 5 ♠   10 ♦ = Q ♣, Q ♠
J ♥ = K ♠, 8 ♣   J ♦ = 3 ♠, J ♣
Q ♥ = 10 ♠, 9 ♣   Q ♦ = 3 ♦, 9 ♦
K ♥ = 2 ♣, 9 ♠   K ♦ = 3 ♣, 7 ♠

A ♣ = 2 ♥   A ♠ = 7 ♥, 2 ♣
2 ♣ = A ♠, K ♥   2 ♠ = 6 ♠, K ♣
3 ♣ = 5 ♦, K ♦   3 ♠ = 6 ♦, J ♦
4 ♣ = 5 ♣, 6 ♥   4 ♠ = 10 ♣, 4 ♥
5 ♣ = 5 ♥, 4 ♣   5 ♠ = 10 ♥, 4 ♦
6 ♣ = 8 ♠, 2 ♦   6 ♠ = 9 ♠, 2 ♠
7 ♣ = 8 ♦, J ♠   7 ♠ = K ♦, 8 ♥
8 ♣ = J ♥, K ♠   8 ♠ = K ♣, 6 ♣
9 ♣ = Q ♥, 6 ♦   9 ♠ = K ♥, 6 ♠
10 ♣ = J ♠, 4 ♠   10 ♠ = 4 ♥, Q ♥
J ♣ = J ♦, 10 ♥   J ♠ = 7 ♣, 10 ♣
Q ♣ = 3 ♥, 10 ♦   Q ♠ = 10 ♦, 8 ♦
K ♣ = 2 ♠, 8 ♠   K ♠ = 8 ♣, J ♥

MY IMPORTANT RELATIONSHIPS

 etermine the relationship cards with significant people in your life and record on this page. Follow the examples below.

EXAMPLES:

Q♣ (25) + Q♦ (38) = 63-52* = 11 or J♥

Q♣ (25) + A♣ (14) = 39 or K♦

*Only subtract from 52 if the combined total of the two cards is larger than 52.

NAME	YOUR SOLAR VALUE		OTHER'S SOLAR VALUE		COMBINED SOLAR VALUE	RELATIONSHIP CARD
_____	_____	+	_____	=	_____	_____
_____	_____	+	_____	=	_____	_____
_____	_____	+	_____	=	_____	_____
_____	_____	+	_____	=	_____	_____
_____	_____	+	_____	=	_____	_____
_____	_____	+	_____	=	_____	_____
_____	_____	+	_____	=	_____	_____
_____	_____	+	_____	=	_____	_____
_____	_____	+	_____	=	_____	_____
_____	_____	+	_____	=	_____	_____
_____	_____	+	_____	=	_____	_____
_____	_____	+	_____	=	_____	_____
_____	_____	+	_____	=	_____	_____
_____	_____	+	_____	=	_____	_____

A ♥ = 1	A ♣ = 14	A ♦ = 27	A ♠ = 40
2 ♥ = 2	2 ♣ = 15	2 ♦ = 28	2 ♠ = 41
3 ♥ = 3	3 ♣ = 16	3 ♦ = 29	3 ♠ = 42
4 ♥ = 4	4 ♣ = 17	4 ♦ = 30	4 ♠ = 43
5 ♥ = 5	5 ♣ = 18	5 ♦ = 31	5 ♠ = 44
6 ♥ = 6	6 ♣ = 19	6 ♦ = 32	6 ♠ = 45
7 ♥ = 7	7 ♣ = 20	7 ♦ = 33	7 ♠ = 46
8 ♥ = 8	8 ♣ = 21	8 ♦ = 34	8 ♠ = 47
9 ♥ = 9	9 ♣ = 22	9 ♦ = 35	9 ♠ = 48
10 ♥ = 10	10 ♣ = 23	10 ♦ = 36	10 ♠ = 49
J ♥ = 11	J ♣ = 24	J ♦ = 37	J ♠ = 50
Q ♥ = 12	Q ♣ = 25	Q ♦ = 38	Q ♠ = 51
K ♥ = 13	K ♣ = 26	K ♦ = 39	K ♠ = 52

The Birth Card has been mathematically calculated
using the following equation:
Double the month of birth, add the day of birth and subtract the sum from 55.
For example if someone's birth date is 2/26
2 x 2 = 4 + 26 = 30. Then 55-30 = 25.
The Solar Value of 25 = Q of Clubs

NAME	YOUR SOLAR VALUE		OTHER'S SOLAR VALUE		COMBINED SOLAR VALUE	RELATIONSHIP CARD
_____	_____	+	_____	=	_____	_____
_____	_____	+	_____	=	_____	_____
_____	_____	+	_____	=	_____	_____
_____	_____	+	_____	=	_____	_____
_____	_____	+	_____	=	_____	_____
_____	_____	+	_____	=	_____	_____
_____	_____	+	_____	=	_____	_____
_____	_____	+	_____	=	_____	_____
_____	_____	+	_____	=	_____	_____
_____	_____	+	_____	=	_____	_____
_____	_____	+	_____	=	_____	_____
_____	_____	+	_____	=	_____	_____
_____	_____	+	_____	=	_____	_____
_____	_____	+	_____	=	_____	_____
_____	_____	+	_____	=	_____	_____
_____	_____	+	_____	=	_____	_____
_____	_____	+	_____	=	_____	_____
_____	_____	+	_____	=	_____	_____
_____	_____	+	_____	=	_____	_____
_____	_____	+	_____	=	_____	_____
_____	_____	+	_____	=	_____	_____
_____	_____	+	_____	=	_____	_____
_____	_____	+	_____	=	_____	_____
_____	_____	+	_____	=	_____	_____
_____	_____	+	_____	=	_____	_____

RELATIONSHIP PATTERNS

ur relationships teach us a great deal. The four charts on the following pages can help you see in your relationships and gain insight and understanding about areas for your challenges and growth.

Once you have identified the relationship cards for yourself and people in your life, place these cards in the appropriate chart. Separate charts for relationships with family members, friends and business associates are provided. Then think about these questions: Do your relationships tend to cluster in one suit? Are certain numbers represented in the same suits or different suits? Are there duplicate cards within your family? Do a parent and spouse have the same card? Is the predominant suit for each area of your life the same or different? Let your mind open to how these cards interconnect.

Once you have completed the relationship patterns cards for family, friends and business associates, record all the relationship cards in the composite chart, under the appropriate suit. This will give you an overview of the larger picture. Are the cards in these major aspects of your life clustered in the same or different suits? Where are the majority of the cards? Is there a suit that is void and empty? There are many more club and diamond people than there are spades and hearts. Are the majority of your relationships in clubs and diamonds or spades and hearts?

Continue to track new relationships as they arise and see if there is a trend in new acquaintances. The combinations of things you can learn is endless.

Family Patterns

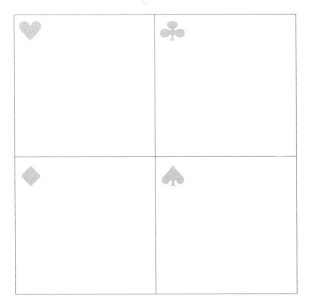

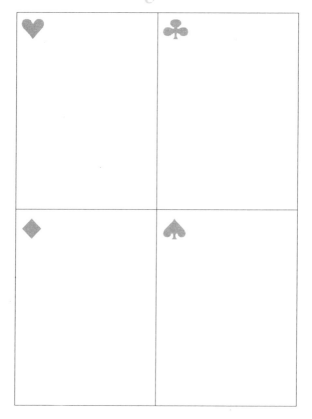

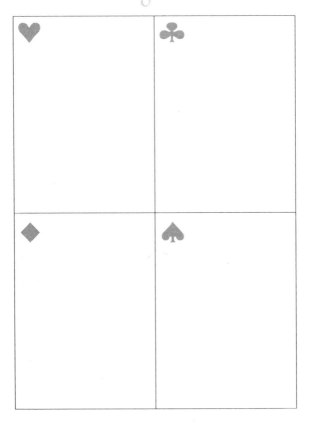

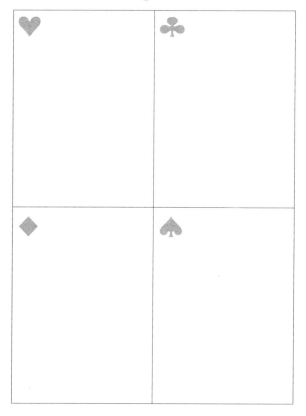

ACE RELATIONSHIPS

 This relationship can be very sweet. Romance, harmony and sensitivity are key aspects. Often this union brings about a new venture, new idea or new information. This relationship has power with business and finances. Traveling together may satisfy any emotional restlessness.

 Sharing information and exploring the curiosities of life are the prime motivating factors of this relationship. In this union you are students of love. Any new information gained will greatly benefit you both. Social activities, working together and travel will add to your variety of experiences.

This relationship greatly explores a new value system for the two of you. This relationship may generate many new ideas. This connection for business may be extremely opportunistic. A love of travel may bring much pleasure. It is important to keep your energies focused and honest.

This relationship is about transformation on all levels. Much can be gained when you learn to release any fears, both emotional and material. Welcome the frequent changes that will come your way. Do not neglect to protect your privacy from outside influences, so as to keep the bond strong.

TWO RELATIONSHIPS

 This is one of the best connections for a relationship, and is often fated. Romance is powerful. This is one of the traditional marriage cards as it represents a strong union of two hearts. New information in regards to matters of the heart often occurs. This is a strong tie for business partnership. Stay focused.

The primary focus of this relationship is cooperation through communication. Common characteristics are fun, creativity, and unusual experiences. New information can flow through this union. Privacy is a priority. This can be an incredibly resourceful connection. Watch the tendency for arguing.

This is an excellent union for business and networking. In this connection, cooperation for the sake of financial security is present. Loyalty is a strong trait. Business involvements may prove to be very successful. People-related activities are very beneficial. Be aware as you may be prone towards codependency.

This relationship represents independence, but is very much about cooperation. Communication is the key to your often fated union. Romance is well aspected. Family often proves to be a common thread for the two of you. It is important not to get in a rut, as you may often make many compromises for the sake of the relationship.

THREE RELATIONSHIPS

 Variety, sociability and drama are characteristics of the relationship. There is an ease in communicating. Work and a solid home base are priorities for success. With this connection you will attract many opportunities to understand your own personal boundaries. Watch for indecision and worry.

This relationship has to do with learning to give on a universal level. Communication is a key influence. It is important to release any negative thought patterns. This is a beneficial connection for any business endeavors. Stay focused.

This connection has the potential for creating much financial versatility. Learning about unconditional love, and not having expectations in relationships are major issues. There is opportunity to master emotions and become more responsible to them. Too many compromises tend to be stagnating.

This is a connection filled with creativity, travel and energy. Each need a partner with whom they can share a variety of activities. Overall there is good marriage potential. Together this union can experience success by directing your focus to intellectual pursuits.

FOUR RELATIONSHIPS

4 HEARTS — *As the marriage card, this is one of the best connections for stability in romance and family. The two of you often have vitality for social activities. Cooperation is an important factor in keeping your foundation strong and protected. Be careful not to get in a rut.*

4 CLUBS — *You can work well together and accomplish much. This relationship can be very constructive and grounding. Satisfaction occurs when you both are focused on the same goals. Creative endeavors will bring you much pleasure. Remember that playing together will bring the balance needed.*

4 DIAMONDS — *Solid values in this union help ground restlessness inherent in the relationship. Financially this connection is very protected when worked for. Traveling is vital to keep this union alive. Public and social involvement may prove to be very effective to both. Be realistic while in love.*

4 SPADES — *This relationship is about building foundations, and a solid sense of home and family. This is one of the better connections for marriage. Conversation is important. There might be a heavy focus on material pleasures, so caution is advised when it comes to spending. Be flexible.*

FIVE RELATIONSHIPS

 Expression and travel are two of the ways the energy moves within this relationship. You may learn from each other about forming boundaries. Satisfaction and rewards come from being emotionally responsible.

This can be a very versatile relationship. Traveling will satisfy your tendency to be restless. Communication on a deep level is transformative and assists in releasing emotional fears. It is important that you recognize the need for each other's privacy and independence. Watch for a inclination towards jealousy.

This relationship is about change, especially in values. Travel or movement of any kind is conducive to maintaining a harmonious union. Versatility is a key word. This is an excellent connection for business ventures. Intellectual stimulation is necessary to keep the relationship alive.

Social activities, romance and travel are conducive to happiness in this relationship and often reduces restlessness. Usually there is protection financially. Many changes regarding your lifestyle will occur as a result of your union. Learn to communicate well and recognize your powerful emotions.

SIX RELATIONSHIPS

6 HEARTS *This relationship has a fated nature about it. Often there is harmony as well as compromises to be made. Home and family are important. Contentment and happiness may result. Be willing to make adjustments to prevent stagnation.*

6 CLUBS *This is a very strong connection that seems fated from the start. Pleasure and sensuality are main ingredients in this relationship. Balancing work and romance is your main challenge, as you can overindulge in both. To avoid a rut, do not take for granted matters of the heart. Watch for illusion and domination in love.*

6 DIAMONDS *Often this relationship is destined. Together social contacts may bring satisfaction. Engaging in physical activities or good conversations may bring rich rewards. Transformation comes from emotional changes. Be careful not to get stuck in a rut.*

6 SPADES *There is a very strong power that brought the two of you together. Compromising is essential as a result of this union. Communicating with each other is the utmost key to your relationship. Together you have a lot of capabilities to create a successful work environment. Be realistic. Avoid being stuck in a rut.*

SEVEN RELATIONSHIPS

7 HEARTS *This relationship is about unconditional love and learning not to have expectations. Traveling together brings many pleasures. By forfeiting personal desires for a higher purpose, overcoming obstacles can be achieved.*

7 CLUBS *Overcoming obstacles through inspiration is sure to bring success in this relationship. This is a strong indicator for satisfaction in love and family. Communication in this connection comes naturally. Fulfillment occurs when working together for humanitarian pursuits. Always keep your sense of humor to help guard against negativity.*

7 DIAMONDS *Material abundance awaits those with this connection if they let go of fears and worry. Much vitality for romance and fun is associated with this union. You may make sacrifices for those you love. Making compromises and adjustments may be your greatest challenge as well as your greatest gift. Be flexible.*

7 SPADES *This is a union of great depth. There is a strong influence of feelings and emotion. There is much to be explored through communicating. You can be very creative when it comes to being resourceful with your finances. This is one of the finest indicators for a solid family and marriage. Remember to be flexible.*

EIGHT RELATIONSHIPS

8 HEARTS   *This can be a very healing relationship and emotionally powerful. Any type of work with groups or the public will be very beneficial and rewarding to you both. Enjoy your friendship as well as your romance. Be patient and disciplined to realize your dreams, To reach your ideals, remember to keep your feet on the ground.*

8 CLUBS   *This is a very powerful relationship. There is a need in this relationship to communicate and express any hidden agendas. Be aware that control and illusion do not hamper the nature of your relationship. There will be restlessness, so expression may be the best safeguard for satisfaction.*

8 DIAMONDS   *This strong connection is about successful values, material and spiritual. You enjoy a variety of pleasures, but emotionally must not scatter your energies. Together you have a lot of vitality to explore new avenues of knowledge and information. Keep your boundaries clear.*

8 SPADES   *This relationship is extremely strong and has the potential to overcome all obstacles. It represents a solid lifestyle. Together you have the opportunity to successfully network in the community. There is opportunity to create profitable business ventures. Beware of control and power issues.*

NINE RELATIONSHIPS

9 HEARTS *This relationship is about abundant giving. Welcome traveling or other changes together, as they bring rich rewards. This relationship could represent a wish fulfilled. Challenges may result around stubbornness and unwillingness to let go of the past.*

9 CLUBS *This relationship can be highly sensual, romantic and fated. It is important that both learn to make compromises and adjustments without losing independence. Your lofty ideals can be unrealistic. To avoid disappointments, be responsible.*

9 DIAMONDS *This is an excellent union for investments and other business related ventures. You welcome travel and changes. You love to communicate, for ill or for good. Marriage and family may prove challenging. Together any humanitarian efforts would be of great service. Be cautious about over-spending.*

9 SPADES *This relationship may produce awakenings and transformations requiring letting go of past ways, habits and viewpoints. It is a strong indication for romance or other heartfelt matters. There is a lot of energy for mastering your values. Do not get carried away with your power.*

TEN RELATIONSHIPS

 This relationship has a lot to do with social activities, travel and inspiration. Youth, the public and new beginnings are keywords. Overcoming all obstacles through the power of love is possible and may lead to your success. Compromise may be required to overcome self-centered behavior.

Communicating and learning from one another are powerful components for mastery in this relationship. This connection desires variety. It is important that there is mental stimulation and a respect for independence. Commitment does not come easy.

This may be one of the greatest financial unions possible. Service of some nature must be incorporated into your lives for material success. Passion on all levels may run high. The relationship may have a lot of ambition for new and creative ways for material gain. Uncertainty may be brought on by emotional restlessness.

 This is the relationship for overcoming and achieving much. You can be very creative financially, and together have the energy for transformation on a very deep level. You may often find yourselves trying to balance family and work.

JACK RELATIONSHIPS

J HEARTS   *This relationship has much to do with serving in love. This can be one of the most steadfast connections, filled with much emotional power and fun. Love is the gift received after many trials. A challenge of this relationship may be inflexibility.*

J CLUBS   *This relationship can be full of inspiration and fun. A lot of vitality comes from conversation and communication. Often seeking answers to the mysteries of life is a common pleasure. Any business endeavors can be very beneficial. Marriage and family are very transformative.*

J DIAMONDS   *This relationship can be inventive, fun and spontaneous in nature. Being resourceful for financial gain may be very productive for you. This union creates much security for those you love. There is a lot of vitality for cooperation. Any traveling you do could bring rich rewards to the relationship. Know when to take off the rose colored glasses.*

J SPADES   *In this relationship you may find yourselves aware of a lifestyle totally different than you have ever known. Communication and humor are big pluses. An element of fun and sociability are characteristic of this relationship. Keep your sense of humor and sense of independence.*

QUEEN RELATIONSHIPS

Q HEARTS *This is one of the key marriage indicators as it represents sweet romance. There is a tendency for strong communication and financial rewards working together. This relationship contains a lot of warmth, gentleness and nurturing. Powerful union, children and the home are key. Watch for idealistic tendencies that could lead to illusions.*

Q CLUBS *This relationship is about service, nurturing and communication on all levels. Balancing values and variety is often a challenge. Welcoming changes may be the spice needed to prevent any monotony. Traveling may help satisfy restlessness.*

Q DIAMONDS *This is a strong influence for business matters. Being open and receptive to higher values may benefit those around you in all matters. Leadership experiences may prove to be your greatest asset. A lot of creativity is available, but staying focused may be a challenge. Be cautious about overspending.*

Q SPADES *This is a very powerful connection. Love and money have difficulty mixing in this relationship. Positive communication is an important element to this relationship. Spontaneous fun may be experienced. It is important to be clear regarding marriage and romance.*

KING RELATIONSHIPS

![K HEARTS] *This is a very loving, powerful and sensual connection. Communication will strengthen your emotional bond. The relationship may present many challenges which if addressed will lead to mastery and maturity. Compromise and adjustment are important considerations. Issues related to control and power may arise.*

![K CLUBS] *This relationship can be very harmonious providing that both individuals have good communication skills. Recognizing interdependence is of great importance to the relationship. This is a strong influence for happiness and success in love or marriage. This powerful connection must release negative ideas, and be realistic.*

 With this union you can influence many with your strong value system. This is a powerful team for working together. When this union comes about, there is often a fated quality, for ill or for good. Be aware of power issues, for the King loves to rule.

 This is the strongest card of the deck. This union may endure many trials and tribulations. Along the way there may be some emotional indecision and uncertainties. There is much potential for wisdom. It is essential to have mutually understood boundaries.

Now Available

YOUR PERSONAL LOVE CARDS REPORT!

In-Depth Relationship Analysis

The purpose of this report is to reveal as much information about you and your partner as possible, using this ancient and highly accurate system. This report will explain many things about you and your partner and how the two of you connect. It typically runs 18-25 typed, colored pages. You will be amazed at what you learn about yourself and what connections you share with your partner — both challenging and full of opportunity! It is intended for opening doors of understanding and awareness.

Fill out the form below and mail it to:

CARDS OF ILLUMINATION

P.O. BOX 770, SEDONA, AZ 86339

TEL: (520) 282-0142 • FAX: (520) 204-1544

Delivery in 7-12 days

PLEASE SEND ME THE LOVE CARDS RELATIONSHIP ANALYSIS
Cost is $30⁰⁰ • Add $1⁵⁰ per report for S&H • (outisde U.S. add $4⁰⁰)

❑ Money Order ❑ Credit Card #_____

Sorry, no checks or American Express Expiration date:_____

First Name:_____ ❑M or ❑F Birthday:_____

First Name:_____ ❑M or ❑F Birthday:_____

(if birthday is on cusp, please indicate which zodiac sign to apply)

Mailing Address:

NAME

STREET   CITY

STATE   ZIP   PHONE

Available Fall 1998

THE COMPLETE CARD READING KIT

This easy, how to kit guides you through the amazing step-by-step process enabling you to shuffle a standard deck of cards, and complete a 13 card reading providing insights for important questions.

✳

THE COMPLETE CARD READING KIT:

DECK OF PLAYING CARDS
SILK CARRY BAG
NUMBERED LAYOUT SPREAD CLOTH
INTERPRETATIONS BOOK

✳

For further information on this system and upcoming workshops, check out our website:
www.cardsofillumination.com
E-mail: cards@sedona.net

CARDS OF ILLUMINATION INC.®

Please contact us
9am - 5pm mst
888-ILLUMN-8
888-455-8668

NOTES

NOTES

NOTES